State to

Reducing a Gap and

BY JOHN PHARMS, AUTHOR AND EDUCATOR

"**What's wrong with Michigan** begs the question for a state that leads the country in unemployment!" — Detroit News, 2009

Michigan is a state that has a 55% black prison population compared to a black population that makes up 14% of its population. Though Michigan does not rank in the top 5% of states who have a large black population enrolled in special education, a great majority of its black citizens would likely be qualified for special education. Detroit is by far the worst of any large city in the country since it will only graduate 25% of their students on average, according to *Detroit News*, October 24, 2007.

Standardizing for All

Michigan's Education Secretary Margaret Spellings echoed her concerns by stating, "In this country today, half of our minority students do not get out of high school on time. That's outrageous!" (*The Associated Press*, October 30, 2008). Spellings goes on to state, "'No Child Left Behind' is largely about grades three through eight. There's not a lot of power in the law as it relates to high schools."

Then what good is that law? If the "No Child Left Behind" law does not reach grades nine through 12, then as a society we're telling those same kids that they are on their own and good luck. *The Associated Press* even mentioned in its National Report on July 27, 2008 that Michigan only graduated 33% of African-Americans compared to 74% of white males. Detroit Public Schools only graduated 25% of its African-American males! What a mess and what a disgrace. Figures for African-American females were not available at the time of this writing. Detroit Public Schools (DPS) needs to reduce this educational gap and standardize a uniform program that will meet the needs of its students.

The Council of The Great City Schools released its findings for the Detroit Public Schools in October 2008. The report, "Reforming & Improving the Detroit Public Schools" is very disturbing for a school district that is marred by disarray and public embarrassment. A June 2009 audit on the state of the Detroit Public Schools is available online by going to www.detnews.com for the full report.

The Detroit Public Schools was in a State takeover from 1999 to 2004 after then-Governor John Engler signed Public Act 10 that paved the way for that takeover. But in 2004, then-Governor Jennifer Granholm signed House Bill 4508, bringing to an end the State takeover of Detroit Public Schools. A number of public schools have been in a state of takeovers for several years, and the latest DPS Audit (Jennifer Mrozowski, *Detroit News*, October 2008) suggests a takeover of DPS's finances is very imminent (please read the June 2009 DPS Audit at www.detnews.com), especially in light of a leveling off of student achievement and enrollment. DPS has had a big student decline as evidence in the 2003-2004 and 2006-2007 reports.

Governor Granholm addressed the State Legislature on February 18, 2009, arguing that there's a need to close between 18 and 52 schools in Detroit due to a lack of enrollment. In 2003, DPS had an enrollment of 150,415 students. When the State of Michigan took over the DPS (1999-2004), Detroit had an enrollment of 108,145, which showed an alarming loss of 38,633 in five and a half years! That's an astounding 7,000 students per academic year. Moreover on continuing this trend, Chastity Pratt Dawson of the *Detroit Free Press* wrote in her September 27, 2008 column that DPS had an enrollment of 88,000 students K-12. So it's even lower in 2008. This jeopardizes DPS its first class district status that will allow private and charter schools to come into Detroit and compete for these vanishing students. But where are these students going, and why the flight?

In 1950, Detroit had a population of 4,467,592 that was due in part to migration from the South to the North by African-Americans who flooded to Detroit because of jobs available in its immense automotive factories. The white flight began in earnest after the Detroit City riots following the assassination of the late Reverend Martin Luther King, Jr. in 1968. To date, DPS is still marred by segregation of its white and black students as those who are able to leave have done so.

The National Negro College Fund, in its drive to raise scholarships, has a commercial which states, "A mind is a terrible thing to waste." Waste? The majority of black crime is black-on-black crime! Where is the outcry of its black church leaders and political leaders? This is where I suggest that everyone go to the internet and download the infamous "Willie Lynch Letter" that was written in the 1700's that encouraged whites to pit different black groups against each other. This article will astound, embarrass and anger its reader because it demonstrates that without any assistance of hate groups, black American men have been systematically eliminating themselves through murder, incarceration, AIDS, and other tragic DBBB (death by being black).

Black churches used to be the focal point of all inner city neighborhoods between the 1940s and the end of the 1970s. It seems now that black inner city leaders are falling victim to greed and shame like their white suburban counterparts. Greed knows no racial or ethnic boundaries. A "see it and claim it" mentality is ruining the black church. Where's the outcry that Johnnie and Debbie can't read

or write? It seems that black leaders express the need to see improvement in test scores, i.e., reading and writing, but little is being done to see those results at the schools.

Author Kati Haycock reflects, "Although everybody wanted to take credit for narrowing the gap of reading, writing and arithmetic, no one wanted to take responsibility for widening it" (Haycock, K., March 2001. Closing the achievement gap. Educational Leadership. 58 (6), 6-11). Even the attempts to end segregation have shown us that students were and are now segregated by race. It seems now that both black and white parents and students are comfortable within their own learning group. Martin Luther King, Jr., John F. Kennedy and Lyndon B. Johnson would be deeply amazed and saddened by this turn of events after their efforts to bring about change through bringing the races together for a better America. That word "change" would later become Presidentelect Barack Obama's theme on his way to becoming the firstever elected African-American President. I might add that since taking office, President Obama has received more death threats than any elected President in the history of this country (National Public Radio, June 19, 2009).

I believe the increase in racial hatred has been fueled today by the way the media, law enforcement, Hollywood, and even hip-hop gangster rap have flamed racial distrust. The "n" word today is as common now as mom's apple pie. Americans view and stereotype the way African-American males will metamorphose into adulthood the way a caterpillar evolves into a butterfly. They believe the majority of these young men will ultimately wind up in the penal system that is overcrowded (200 million and counting) and a breeding ground for higher education amongst the elect of hard-core criminals. In this new millennium, African-American males between the ages of 18-29 can expect to spend most of their early lives in prison.

Most African-Americans see this trend of 18-29 year olds entering this revolving door of a free criminal enterprise because their parents (especially fathers) have been graduates of this hi-tech enterprise where the State of Michigan government spends nearly

$2 billion per year just to keep these criminals incarcerated. I know this as a fact because I was an educator-employee of the Michigan Department of Corrections for nearly ten years.

If we as a society "band-aid" a problem when surgery is required, then the end results will be catastrophic. By failing to provide a quality education, then we're basically telling today's youth that they are disposable trash and as such we as a society no longer need them. We as a society must encourage Generation X to be the best that they can be or we must expect failure to be the name for this group.

When we look at Generation X and what it takes to reduce the gap, the State government is already attempting to rescue these poor and declining inner cities. Again, the June 2009 Audit of Detroit Public Schools (refer to www.detnews.com) is a damning report on what's wrong with the city of Detroit and its students.

> *If we as a society "band-aid" a problem **when surgery is required,** then the end results will be catastrophic.*

Black leaders and parents must demand accountability for their schools and a reason for why they're failing. *The Detroit News* stated that in 2003 only 77% of Michigan students were graduating! On top of that, a whopping 70% of inmates entering prison in 2005 were dropouts. Even more amazing is that 16% of Hispanics and 30% of Blacks between 16 and 24 years of age aren't in school and do not have a high school diploma or a GED. When comparing 2005 to 2009, the increase in Michigan's prison population, and the statistical increase of the African-American and Hispanic prison population, the dropout rate is even more alarming!

Kirk Johnson, Director of Education Police at the Mackinac Center for Public Policy, stated in 2002 all community colleges have remedial courses because one-third of Michigan students graduate leaving high school without the necessary basic skills. The Jackson, Michigan *Citizen Patriot* editorial wrote in its March 16, 2008 editorial that seven in ten students fresh out of high school aren't ready for Jackson Community College courses.

"High schools simply aren't producing students who are college-ready. Colleges are dealing with students who often have been pushed into college without the tools to thrive there. Though students lack these skills, every community college in Michigan is required to accept all students into their colleges, regardless of their lack of basic skills.

The *Jackson Citizen Patriot* in 2005 had an editorial headline, "Higher-Ed Imbalance: Where Are the Males?" Well, a large proportion of the minority males is incarcerated. That's where you can find most of the males in the state of Michigan. In 2005 the *Jackson Citizen Patriot* painted a sad picture in their editorial explaining that 24,300 African-American men are incarcerated while 21,454 African-American men are attending college. Michigan is one of nearly 15 states that have more African-American men in prison than in institutions of higher learning. The failure of our society has already begun.

So, can State government's intervention help resolve this deplorable situation? State initiatives have been rescuing failing schools since 1862 when the Morrill Act created a land grant program to fund state agricultural and mechanical colleges. These same state initiatives were instrumental in establishing land grant programs for science, math, foreign languages, children with disabilities, assistance for drug abuse programs, and school desegregation, based on a landmark decision in 1964.

State accountability, however, is needed now to improve specific indicators of success and common goals. When John Engler was Governor of Michigan from 1996 to 2004 he felt the need to establish a rescue plan to save some of these failing inner city schools such as Flint, Detroit and Benton Harbor to name a few. Appointing financial managers for these schools and others like them is still desperately needed in order for them to have a chance to succeed and not fall victim to political greed and community shame.

The Detroit Public Schools currently finds itself in a similar situation. With another superintendent attempting to rein in a disorganized collection of city leaders and now the resignation of its mayor (who did four months in prison) the Detroit Public Schools is trying to avoid a nightmare of a headache that doesn't seem to be receding. Only five years earlier Detroit was trying to explain its accountability to the State Auditor when funds became conveniently lost. Five Detroit Public Schools workers are being charged with embezzlement after thousands of dollars were found missing. For a full report of the June 2009 audit on the state of the Detroit Public Schools go to www.dnews.com.

*Michigan is one of nearly 15 states that have **more African-American men in prison** than in institutions of higher learning.*

The State Auditor conducted their survey of every Detroit Public School and that audit showed sloppy bookkeeping, employees using school funds for personal loans and missing cash receipts, Emergency Financial

Manager Robert C. Bobb was quoted as saying (June 5, 2009).

Although she had previously rescinded the takeover of Detroit Public Schools, Governor Granholm, on March 19, 2009 initiated an immediate takeover of the city of Pontiac, Michigan, due to the severity of its financial irregularities.

Author and educator James Noll stated that federal policy makers in NCLB failed to wait to address issues such as established laws such as the Civil Rights Act. The American Federal Policy mandated clear standards and demanded results! When those results weren't met, The American Policy Workers, a financial management group that former Governor John Engler set in place while in office, was established to oust corrupt board members, such as those in Flint and Detroit, and replaced them with others who would demand accountability, set clear-cut standards, and insist on immediate results.

Can takeover make a difference? The State of Virginia has shown, with evidence, that accountability systems with concrete goals can change the behavior of its school systems with promising results over a year. Students who attend the Virginia Public School District have benefited by the increased test or improved test scores across the board for all children. Every one of their racial and ethnic groups has also shown improvement in their test scores.

James Noll also noted that resistance to the State accountability system has come from predominately white-affluent suburban neighborhoods. He goes on to say that schools whose students were most likely to do poorly on standard test scores have also been the ones most likely to embrace the new system while other districts in Virginia whose scores are already quite high are those who are fighting the hardest to get rid of this government oversight.

What must be done? State overseers need to work with school systems and to assist them in embracing the need for testing, as they would embrace a school's aspiration for a football championship. Noll says that too many state assessment systems are lacking the resources and vigor. To do this he points out that test scores bounce up and down from year to year for a variety of reasons that are unrelated to actual school performances. Thus, no school system should totally rely on a snapshot of a single year is test scores when making decisions. What Washington governments must avoid—whether state or federal—is simply demanding accountability and walking away!

Teachers across our nation are already arguing over whether school curriculums should be standardized when considering an already widening and diverse student population. California Governor Arnold Schwarzenegger is reviewing eliminating textbooks in favor of the Internet. Nazi Germany also got rid of its books. I believe that eliminating books is not the answer.

> *... accountability systems **with concrete goals** can change the behavior of its school systems with promising results over a year.*

A fellow educator of mine at a Michigan community college admits that the majority of students this individual teacher comes in contact with lack basic reading and writing skills. The Conservative Think Tank Study reported that all community colleges in the United States spend a total of $65.4 million teaching basic skills to students who should have passed these courses before graduating from their local high schools. Public universities spend $18 million while private universities spend a total of $6 million a year. This should not be necessary if the public schools were doing their job.

That same Mackinac Study surveyed more than 100 professional businesses and found that a number of them are spending nearly $2 million a year to teach their workers basic skills in reading, writing and math. That's nearly $92 million!

The State of Michigan alone spends nearly $2.1 billion to keep nearly 47,000 prisoners behind bars and in the latest State Audit, the Michigan Department of Corrections spent $67 million for its 2,390 Correction Officers for overtime. In 2004-05 MDOC spent $67 million and in 2006-07 spent an astounding $77 million. That's a

36% jump (*Lansing State Journal*, October 28, 2008).

"No wonder we can't lure new businesses into Michigan! We don't have the money it would take to lure those potentially new businesses into Michigan because we're spending it to house prisoners and to pay Correction Officers" (*Lansing State Journal*, October 28, 2008).

No one has to tell me that if it looks like a skunk and smells like a skunk then it must be a skunk! Michigan has 11% unemployment rate, which I might add leads the nation. Michigan has a skunk in its house. No one seems to want to admit seeing or smelling the mess we have on our hands.

MAYORAL RESPONSE

Response to this essay from Dave Bing, Mayor of the City of Detroit, after reading this manuscript by John Pharms:

CITY OF DETROIT
MAYOR'S OFFICE

COLEMAN A. YOUNG MUNICIPAL CENTER
2 WOODWARD AVE., SUITE 1126
DETROIT, MICHIGAN 48226
PHONE 313•224•3400
FAX: 313•224•4128
WWW.DETROITMI.GOV

July 10, 2009

John Pharms
3011 North Pointe Drive
Jackson, MI 49202

Dear Mr. Pharms:

Thank you for writing and sharing your thoughts. As promised during my campaign, I take seriously the suggestions, concerns and ideas of those interested in moving Detroit forward.

I've been a Detroiter for the past 42 years, but up until now, I've never been an active politician. In fact, as mayor, I plan to be a statesman, and not a politician. A statesman will tell you the truth, even if it's not popular.

I am interested in advancing Detroit's resurgence – creating a strong foundation for citizens to build good and happy lives for themselves and their family. I have listened to citizens from various Detroit communities and with their input have created a plan that I believe can improve our community and Detroiters' quality of life.

Detroit's challenge is clear; our vision is achievable. I look forward to partnering with individuals, like you, to move Detroit forward. Thank you for joining me – and being a part of the change you wish to see in Detroit.

For Detroit. For Detroiters. For you.

Best Regards,

Dave Bing
Mayor

DB/skb

GOVERNOR'S OFFICE RESPONSE

Response to this essay from Bill Rustem, Director of Strategy with the State of Michigan Executive Office, after reading this manuscript by John Pharms:

RICK SNYDER
GOVERNOR

STATE OF MICHIGAN
EXECUTIVE OFFICE
LANSING

BRIAN CALLEY
LT. GOVERNOR

June 1, 2012

John Pharms
3011 North Pointe Drive, Apt M
Jackson, MI 49202

Dear Mr. Pharms:

    Thank you for your letter to Governor Snyder regarding the gap within the education system and standardization's role in this problem. As the Director of Strategy for Governor Snyder, I am responding on his behalf.

    Within the Executive Office, we are committed to investing in our youth, and continue to develop policies that will better serve our youth and help make Michigan's future brighter. Your thoughts on the matter have been noted, and will be kept in mind as we continue to reinvent Michigan.

    We recognize the talent that our citizens have, and appreciate your concerns. Your expertise and insight is greatly appreciated, and your dedication to Michigan is something that this office also shares in.

Sincerely,

Bill Rustem
Director of Strategy

About the Author
John Louis Pharms

Refusing to accept derogatory labels from society and determined to succeed in an often cruel and unfriendly world, John Pharms, a ward of the court of the State of Michigan since the age of ten months, stands today as a testimony to the virtue of self-determination.

The 6'3", 230-pound former athlete, who today is a retired teacher from the Michigan Department of Corrections, has come a long way from that day more than 50 years ago, when he and his twin brother were made permanent wards of the State after being taken from their natural parents. John Pharms spent many years in institutions, foster care homes, boarding homes, and, at times, in care of his natural aunt and uncle in Grand Rapid, Michigan. Years with mentally- and physically handicapped children was an unpromising start to life that might have depressed and finished many, but not John Pharms.

After receiving his discharge papers from the State of Michigan and graduating from high school, Pharms entered and graduated from Western Michigan University in Kalamazoo, Michigan.

John Pharms then returned to his high school alma mater where he taught and coached athletics in company with some educators who refused to acknowledge that he should ever have been a special education student in the first place. After nearly three years at his alma mater, Pharms decided to take his talents to the university level. Tony Dungy, the former head coach for the Indianapolis Colts football team, referred Pharms (a long-time friend from their high school days in Jackson, Michigan) to Lincoln University in Jefferson City, Missouri (the capital of the state) as an assistant football coach and head resident dorm director. It was here that John Pharms met the late Archie Moore (former light heavyweight boxing champion), through his son Hardy, who resided in the dormitory Pharms directed and played on the Blue Tiger football team. Hardy later passed away from cancer.

After a two-year stint, it was back to the island of Mallorca, Spain, where Pharms had previously done his student teaching. Another two years of coaching, acting as the schools athletic directory, and being house-father for the boys' dormitories, and it was yet again time for Pharms to meet a new challenge. This time it was Arhus, Denmark.

A Christmas visit to his Danish family where he had lived as an exchange student, prompted Pharms to tackle European professional basketball and teach in the Danish school system. A couple years of coaching, as well as teaching physical education and American history classes, and it was back to the States, even though Pharms passed up an opportunity to coach European basketball, turning down a contract offer from Poland.

A brief stint in Michigan, and Pharms was off to Raleigh, North Carolina, where he was head supervisor of a dry cleaning establishment in the small town of Ajax. After a year there, he decided to visit a friend from his coaching days in Denmark, who lived on Cap Cod, Massachusetts. John Pharms went for a two-week visit and stayed nearly five years. While there, he worked in a program called Latham School for the Mentally Challenged, where he also won a part in the old television series, *Unsolved Mysteries*.

Back in Michigan again, Pharms received his Masters degree from Spring Arbor University and taught for over a decade for the Michigan Department of Corrections, John Pharms has won numerous accolades, including being nominated in his hometown for the Citizen of the Year award due to his many years of volunteer service reaching that town's inner-city youth.

Though John Pharms has never been married and at 60 years of age, has never had any children, he has found time to give back to society many "thank you's" for having given him the opportunity to accomplish so much after so much was denied him.

www.ingramcontent.com/pod-product-compliance
Lightning Source LLC
Chambersburg PA
CBHW040916180526
45159CB00010BA/3092